BUILDING BLACK WEALTH

SIMPLE AND POWERFUL STEPS THAT BLACKS CAN TAKE IN ORDER TO BUILD WEALTH

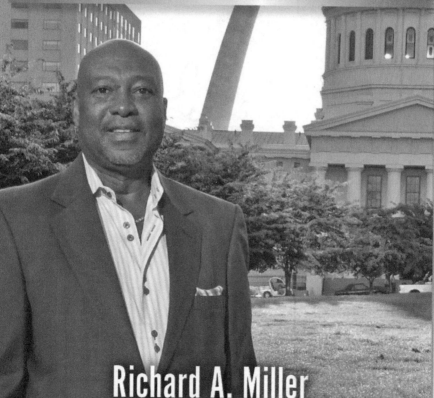

Richard A. Miller

This Signed copy of

Building Black Wealth
Simple and Powerful Steps that Blacks Can Take in Order to Build Wealth

by

Go Get that Chedda! $$$

Richard A. Miller

Is part of a limited special edition bound by the publisher.

This Book Is Dedicated to:

My Parents: Hiram and Jasmine Miller and

My Godmother: Mrs. Iona King

(Who gave me a Wonderful Childhood)

May you rest in peace.

My Loving Wife: Gwen who Supports me, and My Children:

Shardé and Jamal who Inspire me.

Building Black Wealth
Simple and Powerful Steps that Blacks Can Take in Order to Build Wealth

~

Copyright © 2021 by Richard A. Miller, MBA & Former Car Dealer

Email: WealthBuildingForBlacks@gmail.com

Website: www.WealthBuildingForBlacks.com

ISBN: 9781734916546

Library of Congress Control Number: 2022902196

Contributors
Editor: Jana Thomas
Photographer: Multimedia Publications, Lamont Shannon
Graphic Designer: Elaine A. Young - www.HopscotchCommunications.com

BUILDING BLACK WEALTH

TABLE OF CONTENTS

INTRODUCTION | VIII
FOREWARD | XI

CHAPTER	PG
1	FICO Is Your Friend: Raise Your Credit Score!	1
2	Be Thrifty in the beginning while you save Cash $$$	6
3	Live Rent-Free & Purchase Rental Properties with the Money you Save	10
4	Impediments to Building Wealth	14
5	The Student Loan SCAM	19
6	Using Stock Market Gains to Build Wealth	22
7	Consider a Career or Investments that Pays Residual Income	33
8	How will a Natural Disaster like (COVD-19) Affect Your Wealth?	35
9	Jobs - Vs - Trades and Self-Employment	37
10	Protect your assets and Build Generational Wealth with Insurance	39
11	Using Reverse Mortgages to Enjoy Life & Pass on Wealth	42
12	Reclaiming Your Parents or Your Grandparents Land	45
13	Start A Business - (Blacks Need More Businesses!)	47
14	Estate Planning: Trusts, Wills, Deeds, TOD's, Beneficiary Assignments	50
15	Succession Plans	54
16	Paying Taxes to Uncle Sam	58
17	Building Your Real-Estate Team	61
18	Recapping	67
19	Giving Back by Becoming a Black Mentor	70
Biography	72
African American Homeownership Statistics	74
Bibliography	79

INTRODUCTION

During the American Civil War, African Americans were promised 40 acres and a mule as a part of "Special Field Order, No. 15", issued on January 16, 1865, by General William T. Sherman[1]. This field order set aside a large swath of land along the coast of South Carolina, Georgia, and Florida (400,000 acres of Prime Real-Estate) for the exclusive settlement of approximately 18,000 formerly enslaved Black families, and other Blacks living in the area. The order was intended to address the problem of dealing with the tens of thousands of Black refugees and Black soldiers who had joined and assisted the Union Army.

After President Abraham Lincoln was assassinated, his vice president Andrew Johnson, who was never in favor of field order No. 15, assumed the presidency and quickly rescinded the order. Had field order No. 15 been implemented, Blacks in America would have had a solid foundation, on which we could build wealth.

During reconstruction, many Blacks and Black farmers worked tirelessly, saved their income and purchased land in the south. Due to a host of problems with deeds and titles, many of which were manufactured by jealous people with decision-making positions in the County Administration offices, and the USDA (US Dept of Agriculture), many Blacks lost their land and their farms, wiping out a significant amount of generational wealth. For decades after Field Order No.15 and reconstruction, Blacks in America have struggled to build wealth, and pass that wealth on to our children.

This book "Building Black Wealth" clearly defines wealth, and it also discusses <u>economic leakage</u>. Economic leakage is the process of blacks spending $1.4Trillion every year, outside of our communities, with folks who don't look like us.

Building wealth is a mindset. The sooner you embrace that mindset in life and explain it to your children and your grandchildren, the sooner that mindset will become a part of you and your family's DNA, which can be passed on for generations. Jewish families have embraced this mindset for centuries.

This book provides a road map that the average Black person can use to build wealth. There's something in it for people of all ages and cultural backgrounds. It's written very simply, not to be condescending to those of you who may have MBAs and PhDs, but so that both young adults and seniors can read, understand what they're reading, and most importantly implement some of the step by step suggestions in order to build wealth.

Despite the setback of not receiving our 40 acres and a mule 157 years ago, which would have given us a significant leg up on building wealth in America, there are still several opportunities for the average African American to use today to build wealth. One of the most common wealth building strategies is investing in real-estate.

Receiving passive income every month from renters is a beautiful thing! Since God is making no more land on earth, land is a very valuable commodity. Its value is reflected all the way back to biblical times. God led Moses and the Jews to the promised *land*, which was often referred to as the land of milk and honey. So, if you don't own any land, please make it a point to acquire some as soon as possible.

Since the demand far outpaces the supply, the value of land and real-estate will always increase with time.

Some of us have squandered opportunities to keep land that was passed down to us by our parents and grandparents. We didn't take the time, or we didn't know how to properly title the land, secure the deeds, pay the taxes, or remove any liens in order to maintain that land. As a result, the land was auctioned off, or in some cases, taxes have piled up and the land remains unclaimed.

If you have land that was willed to you or your parents, but that land was never legally claimed, it may be worth it to do some research to determine how you can claim your land. If there are future plans to develop that land, or land surrounding yours, depending on the time-frame of those plans you may be able to sell your land to developers and make a nice profit. If it's a long-term plan, your children or grandchildren could reap the benefits of your decision to secure your family land.

Investing in real estate, and securing passive income is one of the easiest ways that almost anyone can utilize, in order to build wealth. If real-estate is not for you, then find a career or investments that pays residual income, or start a small-business.

This book will illustrate various actions you can take in order to build wealth. If you're already wealthy, this book wasn't written for you. Although it may help you grow and retain your wealth. This book was written for young adults starting out, and for your Aunt Mary and your Cousin Pookie, who always seem to be "Broke and Skruggling!" (We all have one of them in our families).

The book presents simple and practical steps anyone can use to build wealth. Ultimately, you will have an opportunity to create generational wealth by passing it on to your children and your grandchildren. If you're a spiritual person, check out: Proverbs Chapter 13 verse 22, "A good man leaveth an inheritance to his children's children". On your way to building wealth, please don't forget to give to your <u>Church</u>, your <u>Local Charity</u>, and<u> to the Poor</u>. "It will come back to you "Tenfold"!

FOREWARD

In his second book **Building Black Wealth** Rich Miller provides simple and clear information on how to build personal and generational wealth. He gives you step by step instructions for wealth development and shows how he used those principles in his own life. Due to removal of courses in fundamental economics, business development and things like banking, many young people today have little exposure to the principles of wealth development. Often times the information provided in this book is never made explicit to many segments of the population. Miller's book is written in plain straight forward easily digestible language. What makes this book more interesting is that Miller uses his own life & financial experiences as examples, so he actually shows how the principles he suggests work in "real" life. He discusses the importance of planning, sacrifice and organization. But he also stresses the fact that everyone can develop a wealth portfolio and it is never too early or late to do it no matter who you are.

Miller isn't trying to sell the readers anything, he is trying to empower people to take control of their own lives and financial destiny. With this book Miller is giving back to the community, by passing along the "entrepreneurial spirit" he received from his parents. This book is a must read for every young adult and anyone wishing to improve their financial condition. Although the book is called Building *Black* Wealth the information outlined in the book is useful for all populations wishing to develop their wealth portfolios.

Dr. Sharon Squires

Associate Professor Sociology, Lincoln University, Missouri

Chapter 1

FICO IS YOUR FRIEND
(Raise your credit score)

FICO, Fair Isaac Corporation - Bill Fair (an engineer) and Earl Isaac (a mathematician) founded the FICO Corporation in 1956 to provide an industry-standard for creditworthiness. In 1991 FICO Scores were released to the 3 credit bureaus (Experian, Equifax, and TransUnion)[2].
   Your FICO score can be viewed as a summary of your credit report. Please go to myFICO.com, and research your FICO Score. They're the ones who developed the score, and 90% of lenders use it.

It's based on your outstanding debt, the amount of credit you've been extended by your creditors, how much of that credit you've used, and how timely you pay your bills. A FICO Score allow lenders to make a quick decision on who they will loan money to.

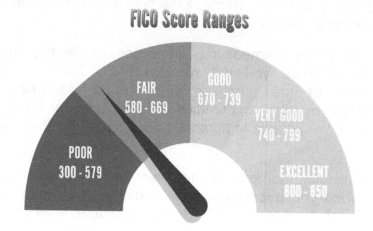

FICO Score Ranges

FAIR
580 - 669

GOOD
670 - 739

VERY GOOD
740 - 799

POOR
300 - 579

EXCELLENT
800 - 850

FICO Score Ranges:

Poor: 300 - 579

Fair: 580 - 669

Good: 670 - 739

Very Good: 740 - 799

Excellent: 800 - 850

A good credit score gives you leverage. It allows you to purchase a big ticket item like a house or a car with little cash down, and receive a low interest rate.

The lower your FICO Score, the less credit you will be offered, and your interest rate will be higher, resulting in higher monthly payments. A high FICO score (700 to 850) shows credit worthiness and will result in lower interest rates. The sooner you establish your credit history, pay your bills on time and raise your FICO score, the quicker you will be able to purchase a house.

The 1st step in building personal wealth - homeownership will allow you to build equity, and avoid wasting money by renting. For most first-time home owners, your mortgage will be lower than the rent you would normally pay for an apartment, or the money you would spend to rent a house. As a result, you can now save more money, and build equity in the house that you own, which increases your wealth.

As a first-time homeowner, in order to qualify for an FHA Home loan, you will need a FICO Score of 580+, and 3.5% of the purchase price as a down-payment[3]. The sooner you raise your credit score, and save some cash, the sooner you will be able to purchase your home and start building wealth.

As an investor, homeownership also increases your wealth; it also gives you **passive income**, which is the rental income that you acquire every month from your renters, without having to do much. Additionally, your job may require that you have a car. Good credit will allow you to purchase that car and receive a good interest rate on your car loan, giving you an affordable monthly payment. A good credit score will also help you down the road, if you decide to start a business.

In order to raise and maintain a high credit score, it's important that you limit the amount of debt that you take on. Your overall debt to income ratio has to be 43% or lower, in order to get approved for an FHA Home Loan. Most lenders want that ratio to be "below 40%", so please limit your student loan debt, your credit card debt, and all of your other outstanding debt. Lenders look at two DTI (Debt to Income) ratios, before approving mortgage loans.

Frontend DTI & Backend DTI

If your income is $3,000/ Month:

While your monthly expenses are the following: $860/month for mortgage, $67/month for annual home insurance ($800/year), $125/month for property taxes ($1,500/year), $20/month for HOA fees ($240/year), $350/month for vehicle note ($4,200/year), $400/month for student loans ($4,800/year), and $200/month for credit card payments ($2,400/year.)

Your **Housing Cost** will be **$1,072** ($860+ $67+ $125+ $20) – giving you a **Frontend-DTI** or **Housing Ratio** of **35.7 %** ($1,072 divided by $3,000.) Lenders want that ratio to be **31% or less**[4].

Your **Total Monthly Housing and Debt payments** will be **$1,822** ($1,072 + $400 + $200) - giving you a **Backend-DTI** of **60.7 %** ($1,822 divided by $3,000.) Lenders want that ratio to be **57% or lower**, in order to qualify for an FHA Loan.

In order to improve your ratios, you will have to either raise your income, perhaps by adding a part time job, or reduce your student loan payments and your credit card payments. Student loan debt & credit card debt are the main culprits preventing young people from building wealth at an early age!

Credit Score Models:

There are several models that creditors use in order to determine your credit score. That's why if you go to buy a house, your credit score may be different from your score at the car dealership, when you go to buy a car.

Your mortgage broker and your car dealer may be using different credit score models. One of the most commonly used models is the VantageScore 3.0 model. This model relies on 6 Factors which influence your score.

1- Payment History – 40%

2- Credit History – 21%

3- Credit Usage – 20%

4- Total Balances – 11%

5- Credit Checks – 5%

6- Available Credit – 3%

Other models may weigh these 6 factors differently.

You can go to: <u>www.creditsesame.com</u> to gather more information on the VantageScore 3.0 model and how it works.

<u>Summary</u>: Steps to Improve your Credit and Raise your FICO Score.

1. Pay your bills on time.

2. Don't borrow money that you can't repay.

3. Do not *max out* your credit cards or your revolving credit. Only use 30% of your allotted credit.

4. Avoid credit inquiries if possible.

5. Avoid bankruptcies & foreclosure.

6. Review your credit report quarterly, and write letters to the 3 bureaus challenging inaccurate information on your reports. Ask them to remove it.

7. Make sure that your creditors are reporting your monthly payments.

8. Prepare a monthly budget including all of your expenses. Consider getting a part time job if your expenses exceed your income.

Several years of paying rent for an apartment, while also paying off your high student loan and credit card debt, can prevent you from saving money and lowering your ratios to purchase that first home (all while building your landlord's wealth.)

Unfortunately, in order to speed up the process, you may have to either increase your income by getting another job, adding a part time job, getting a roommate to pick up half of your rent and utilities, or heading back home to live with your parents for a few years while you reduce your debt and save some cash.

Remember, *FICO is your friend* – so please raise your FICO score.

Chapter 2

Be Thrifty in the Beginning While You Save Cash $$$

Simply put, wealth is the money you save and the assets you accumulate that grow in value as time goes by. Those savings and assets can also be passed on to your children or your loved ones down the road. Building wealth, can also allow you to:

(a) improve the current quality of your life (b) accomplish the things on your bucket list sooner rather than later and (c) accumulate the income that you will need to enjoy your retirement and/or fund your long-term care.

Unfortunately, many of us have never been taught how to build wealth at an early age. Some of us have figured it out later on in life. The sooner you start to acquire wealth, the sooner you will enjoy the quality of life you desire and deserve.

Personal homeownership is the first step in building wealth. Passive income from owning rental properties, residual income and additional streams of income from owning a small business or other business endeavors, gains from the stock market – these are other ways of building wealth which we will explore later on in this book.

In the beginning, building wealth will require some discipline on your part. You will have to develop the discipline of being thrifty, which will allow you to save cash for the purchase of your first home, or cash you will need to start your own business.

I acquired my discipline as a teenager at the age of 14, when I made $42.84 a week on a summer Job. I saved 25% of that income, and throughout my early adulthood as I made more money; I continued to save 25% of my gross income. At the age of 33, as a result of saving and investing, I accumulated $150,000 which I used as seed money to start my first business.

If you're a young adult, you will have to start saving and resist the urge of constantly spending cash, because you will derail your goal of becoming wealthy. You will also have very little cash for that rainy day which is right around the corner in the form of getting laid off, car problems, emergencies, pandemics, medical bills. Saving is extremely difficult for young adults who love nice things. When you get that urge to spend, remember that you can buy even nicer things when you become wealthy.

If you're still having difficulty controlling your urge to spend, find a couple of thrift shops in the wealthiest sections of your city. Wealthy people donate designer shoes and clothing, art, jewelry, appliances, furniture, and lots of nice stuff, that you can purchase and save thousands of dollars. Purchase that stuff, have it dry cleaned, and go about your business in style with cash in the bank. If you're a teenager, go get a part time job, preferably in sales, if possible.

Open a savings account and save 25% of your income. You'll be doing this for several reasons: (a) you'll embrace the independence of having your own cash at an early age, (b) you can purchase your own stuff without having to ask your parents for money, and (c) you'll develop the discipline of saving at an early age. (d) A job interacting with people will allow you to enhance your interpersonal skills at an early age.

If that job is in sales, it will also help you develop your sales skills and confidence at a very early age. These are skills that you will need throughout your lifetime. They will set you apart from your peers, and allow you to be successful. In order to be thrifty, in the beginning you will have to avoid buying new stuff. Buy used! If you need a bicycle, a computer, a camera, CD's, TV's, you can purchase them at thrift shops or pawn shops. Never buy a **brand-new** car unless you can get 0% financing and a large ($4,000 to $8,000) rebate[5]. Please take this advice seriously, I once owned a new car dealership. From my experience, as soon as you drive that new car off of the lot, it will depreciate by thousands of dollars. You're better off purchasing a used car with some warranty left on it (preferably one coming off of a manufacturer's lease) or one that was auctioned by a rental car agency.

If you detail one of those cars having 15,000 to 30,000 miles on it and set it next to a new one, no one will be able to tell the difference. If you like that new car scent, it comes in a bottle. You can purchase it from any car wash, and spray it all over your car. By purchasing that used car, you will save upwards to $10,000 or more. When purchasing a car, never finance for more than 4 or 5 years.

Most car warranties are 5 years/60,000 miles, whichever comes first. So, if you finance for more than 5 years, you will be making monthly payments on a car with no warranty. If you have to replace the engine or transmission ($3,500 to $5,000) depending on the brand, you will not be a happy camper having to make monthly payments on a car that you can't drive.

For more detailed information on how to purchase a car, please refer to my book, **Dealing** (available on Amazon.com or Barnesandnoble.com).

Become thrifty, shop at farmers markets instead of the local grocery stores. You can walk away with two large shopping bags of fruits and vegetables for under $20, and you will avoid unhealthy canned goods. If you have to make that trip to the grocery store, purchase chicken and fish instead of that expensive steak. It's cheaper, and health wise it's better for you. In the rare instances that you have to purchase can goods, get the store brand. It's cheaper and it probably came from the same batch as the brand name product.

With the money you saved from being thrifty, set aside an emergency fund that's enough to cover all of your living expenses for at least 3 months, in the event that you lose your job, get laid off, or become sick or incapacitated and can't work. Borrowing money to cover your living expenses, will put you in a hole that's very difficult to get out of.

Avoid payday loans and title loans altogether! They should be illegal. The 25% to 35% interest that you have to pay on those loans, will set you back even further.

If the income from your job will not allow you to cover your living expenses (rent, food, utilities, telephone, gas, insurance, savings) then you either need to change jobs (getting one with more income), or you need to add a part time job. **Note:** that I included savings in your living expenses. With your new mindset, your savings now becomes an expense. Paying that expense is just as important as paying rent, your insurance, or any of your other expenses. My dad always said, "When paying your bills, pay yourself first!"

Throughout the early stages of your working life, make sure that you pay your bills *on time.* You're building your credit, that you will need real soon. You don't want to build the wrong type of credit. Bad credit, will severely limit your ability to get off to a fast start in building wealth, and you will waste a whole lot of time trying to clean it up.

Avoid credit cards. It's good to have one for emergencies but please don't get into the habit of constantly using it, you need to establish the discipline of saving that we discussed earlier. Credit cards will derail that discipline, and prevent you from saving.

Chapter 3

Live Rent-Free & Purchase Rental Properties with the Money you Save

After you've accumulated your emergency fund, and you've built up your savings, consider purchasing a two-family home in an affordable part of your city. By putting 20% down on the purchase, you will avoid paying PMI (Private Mortgage Insurance.) If you don't have 20% which would be ($20,000) on a $100,000 home, go ahead and put the minimum $3,500 (3.5%) down and pay the PMI. Since your first home will be a 2-family home, the rent you collect from your tenant will be enough to cover your mortgage, PMI, property taxes, and your monthly home-owners insurance.

By renting one side of your two-family home to a well screened tenant. You will now live rent free, allowing you to save some serious cash. Depending on the average rent is your area, you may be allowed to charge enough rent to cover your monthly utilities as well, allowing you to save almost your entire paycheck. If you can't find a 2-family home for under $100,000 in your area, purchasing two single family homes for under $70,000 each, will have a similar effect.

Make sure that each house comes with 3 bedrooms and 2 bathrooms. In the event that we experience another pandemic, or a recession, and you're unable to find a working tenant, your local Housing Authority is always looking for: 3bed/ 2bath homes for their Section – 8 program. They will pay you (estimated) $1,000/ month rent, for a nice 3bed/ 2bath home, depending on the area.

Mortgage Payment Example:

(Using **www.nerdwallet.com** free PMI Calculator.)[6]

Zip Code: 63136

Purchase Price: $100,000

Down Payment: $3,500 (3.5%)

Interest Rate: 4.5%

Mortgage Insurance (PMI) rate: 0.5%

(Typically range from 0.58% to 1.86% depending on: your Credit Score, Loan-to-Value (LTV) Ratio, and Debt-to-Income (DTI) ratio.)

Loan Term: 30 Years

Results:

Monthly PMI: $40

Total PMI: $4,260

(The total amount of PMI you'll pay until you reach 20%equity)

Monthly Cost Breakdown:

Principal and Interest: $489

PMI: $40/Month

Property Taxes (Est): $83/Month

Homeowners Insurance: $43/Month

Total: $655/ Month

After living in that 2-family house rent free for two years, you should have saved enough cash and increased your credit score enough to repeat the cycle. Purchase another 2-family home, this time in a better area. Rent out both units of the first house, and again live in the newer home rent free for two more years. At the end of six years, you will own three 2-family homes with five people paying you rent every month, while living rent free. The income from your renters is called **passive income**. You'll receive it every month like clockwork.

If you can't find 2-family homes in your area for under $100,000, go ahead and purchase single family homes. Make sure that you purchase them for under $70,000 each, and again they should all have (3beds/ 2baths). *Three & Two's* are easier to rent and sell. Section 8 is always looking for them.

If you live in a city like New York or Los Angeles, finding 2 family homes under $100,000 may be difficult. However, with the Internet and Zillow.com, there's absolutely no reason why you can't search for those houses online and hire an agent in St. Louis, or in Houston, to help you purchase them. You can download DocuSign on your cell phone or iPad and sign all of the required documents at your home in (New York or Los Angeles) in order to facilitate your purchase.

There's a huge demand for single family homes with 3 bedrooms and 2 bathrooms. The Housing Authority Section-8 programs across the country, has a long waiting list for 3 bedroom and 4 bedroom homes, and depending on the condition and the area, they will pay $1,000+/ Month, to landlords who rent them to needy families.

At closing, or every 3 months you can fly into St. Louis or Houston, inspect your properties, do some cosmetic repairs (paint/ change filters/change locks/plant roses, etc.), and check out homes that are up for sale with your agent. Then, use 100% of your air travel expenses and hotel expenses as a business tax write off. You can even take your agent to dinner and go to an R&B or rap concert afterwards and use

50% of the cost of your meals and your concert tickets as a meals and entertainment business tax write-off as well.[7]

Now that you have some passive income and some breathing room, consider changing your job, or adding a part time job that will pay you **residual income**, which is income that you receive every month from every item that you've ever sold.

For example, I currently own an insurance agency, StoneLeaf Finance & Insurance Group (www.stoneleafinsurance.com) and I receive monthly income from policies that I sold over 12 years ago. As long as my clients are alive, and continue to keep their policies, those residual checks will be deposited into my checking account every month like clockwork. People pay their life insurance, health insurance, house insurance, and car insurance, every month before buying food.

Gaining passive income and residual income are two of the simplest ways to build wealth. Anyone can acquire those two revenue streams with just a little effort.

Chapter 4

Impediments to Building Wealth

Now that you've survived 6 years of being thrifty, and you've become a real estate mogul, it's time to treat yourself and splurge a little. Take a vacation, go on a cruise (if the pandemic subsides), relax on a beach while sipping on one of those cocktails (with the little umbrella!) Reflect on what you've accomplished over the past six years, and think about what you would like to accomplish over the next 6 years. Set some goals, and consider starting a business.

On the other hand, if you were not successful in getting off to a fast start, there's a good chance that your failure was a result of one or more of the following impediments to building wealth:

1. Fear of Failure

2. Lack of Motivation

3. Laziness

4. Bad influences or a Reluctant Spouse

5. Self Doubt

6. Bankruptcy or Foreclosure

7. Student Loan Debt

8. Bad Credit and a Low FICO Score

Fear of Failure:

This is probably the number one reason why people never set goals, pursue dreams and accomplish their dreams. They're afraid of failing!

Most successful people have failed, and many have failed several times. There's no shame in failing. In fact, the positive side of failure is the fact that you had the courage to try something new and you gained knowledge and experience in the process. Courage, knowledge and experience are positive things that will help you become successful eventually. So, don't be afraid of failure!

Lack of Motivation:

I don't know about you, but the thought of being poor for the rest of my life, the thought of having no control over my life, the thought of always being stressed out, the thought of not being able to do the things I like to do, go to the places I like to go to, eat the foods I like to eat - those are scary thoughts that give me a whole lot of motivation!

Laziness:

Some days we all get the urge to just sit around and read a book, or relax and do absolutely nothing. Or, we may want to recover from a stressful week, or from physically overworking our bodies with manual labor or exercise. However, if you constantly get the urge to just sit around doing nothing! Your laziness, and lack of motivation may be tied to depression or to other psychological or physical issues of which I'm not equipped to discuss. You may need to seek professional care from a psychologist or a physician.

Bad Influences or a reluctant spouse:

This is a tricky one. I'm not going to tell you to leave your family and friends, or to leave your spouse. However, if your friends are encouraging you to quit work or school to hang out, which could cause you to lose your job, lose your income, or get a failing grade at school. At some point, you have to decide what's important to you. Do you want to accomplish your dreams? Are you mentally strong enough to say NO to your family and friends? Do you have the discipline to fight peer pressure?

Does your spouse encourage you to pursue your dreams or does he or she constantly promote negativity and self-doubt? At some point you may have to compromise. Your spouse may not want to live in the part of the city that will allow you both to live rent free in a 2-family home, saving lots of cash. However, if you find that you're the only one willing to compromise - that's not a healthy relationship. Your spouse may be derailing your goals and your dreams.

Self-Doubt:

Self-Doubt is a natural reaction whenever we venture into something new. Do I have the correct information? Do I have enough skills to pull this off? Do I have enough resources to help me with my decision? Do I have the cash required to get started? Once you receive answers to those questions, your doubt will dissipate, and you will have more confidence in accomplishing your goal. If you're still in doubt, keep asking more questions and keep educating yourself. Eventually, you will come to the realization that (a) You can pull it off, or (b) you're not ready – you need more skills, more resources, or more cash.

Bankruptcy or Foreclosure:

Bankruptcy and Foreclosure are *last resort* options that can derail your goals of building wealth for a long time. Bankruptcies stay on your credit report for 7 to 10 years, hurting your chances of qualifying for a mortgage or other credit. As a rule of thumb, some lenders may require a waiting period of 7 years before a foreclosed homeowner can apply for a new mortgage.

As a result, before you make these drastic choices you should consult with an expert or attorney, and explore all available options to avoid standing on the sidelines for 7 to 10 years. If you're 62 years or older, and you're faced with foreclosure issues, consider a reverse mortgage. The only requirements are: that you are 62+, have some equity in your home, and that you continue to pay your taxes, insurance and maintenance.

A reverse mortgage will allow you to: (a) payoff the existing mortgage balance on your home (and you will no longer have a mortgage payment) (b) pull some equity out while continuing to live in your home. You can use that equity to go on a vacation, purchase a car, or do whatever you desire with your cash. Most importantly, a reverse mortgage allows you to avoid foreclosure which can ruin your credit and derail your opportunities to build wealth.

Student Loan Debt:

Unfortunately, it's very difficult to file bankruptcy and discharge yourself from student loan debt. In most cases, it stays with you for life! With such dire consequences, before taking on student loan debt, you **MUST** ask yourself the following questions: Is my degree worth the debt I'm about to take on? How much income will I generate as a result of my degree? Will the income I generate from my degree allow me to pay off my debt while I save and build wealth? Or will I simply be paying the interest on my loan? How long will it take me to pay off my debt based on my current income? How long will it take me based on my current income, to have a 43% Debt to Income Ratio, so that I can qualify for an FHA Loan? What are the alternatives to taking on this debt? Like grants? Scholarships? Less expensive community college tuition? Company paid tuition? Teach for America graduate tuition? Will my degree give me the skills I need to accomplish my career goals? Will my degree assist me in ultimately building wealth?

Bad Credit and Low FICO Scores:

Bad credit and low FICO Scores will prevent creditors from extending you credit, or loaning you cash. As a result, you will have no leverage. You will wind up spinning your wheels and wasting a whole lot of time; some of you will be stuck in poverty. Bad credit and low FICO Scores are things you can control. Don't borrow money that you (a) don't have the ability to repay, or (b) that you have no intention of repaying. Simply put, don't live beyond your means. If you can't pay your bills on time, you either have to:

- Get a new job paying you more income.
- Get a part time job to generate additional income, or eliminate some of the expenses and debt that you're having difficulty paying off.
- You may have to go without Cable TV for a while. You may have to cook your meals instead of eating out. You may have to eliminate your internet bill, by using free Wi-Fi at Starbucks. Be sure to pay your bills on time and build your credit score. The sooner you do, the sooner you will be able to build wealth.

Homeownership allows you to build equity in something you own. Renting wastes your hard-earned income. Living rent free in a 2-family home by using your tenant's rent to pay your mortgage is one of the quickest and most effective ways of building wealth. You won't be able to purchase that 2-family home, if you have poor credit, and a low FICO Score.

Chapter 5

The Student Loan SCAM

In 2021, the average student loan debt was $37,172 and the average student loan payment was $393/month. In order to qualify for an FHA mortgage, your Debt to Income ratio has to be below 40%. We all know that homeownership is the first step in building wealth, so the sooner you purchase your first home, the sooner you will be on your way to building wealth. I know the importance of a good education. Moreover, I know the pressure to go to college that young people face. However, before you take on an enormous amount of debt that can ruin your life, remember, it's very difficult to file bankruptcy to discharge student loan debt. Before you sign for that student loan that could keep you in debt for a long time, derailing your efforts to build wealth, please ask yourself the following **8 questions** regarding student loan debt:

1. Is my degree worth the debt I'm about to take on?

2. How much income will I generate as a result of my degree?

3. Will the income I generate from my degree allow me to pay off my debt while I save and build wealth? Or will I simply be paying the interest on my loan?

4. How long will it take me to pay off my debt based on my current income?

5. How long will it take me based on my current income, to have a 43% Debt to Income Ratio, so that I can qualify for an FHA Loan?

6. What are the alternatives to taking on this debt? Like grants? Scholarships? Less expensive community college tuition? Company paid tuition? Teach for America graduate tuition?

7. Will my degree give me the skills I need to accomplish my career goals?

8. Will my degree assist me in ultimately building wealth?

Every high school senior should consider these 8 questions before signing a contract that has the potential to negatively impact his or her life. Think about it, if the **Average Student Loan Debt** is **$37,172**[8], and you only make **$63,645**[9] as a school teacher (national average for school teachers in the 2019-2020 school year) or **$51,760**[10] as a social worker (national average for social workers in 2020), your DTI ratio would be very high.

With just your student loan debt (no credit cards or other debt), your Debt to Income (DTI) Ratio will be – (58.4% as a School Teacher) and (71.8% as a Social Worker). The FHA requirement is 43% or Lower. Although teaching and social work are honorable professions that should be rewarded by society, you will be denied homeownership for a long time. You will have to carry that student loan albatross around your neck, until you lower your DTI ratio. If you purchase a car or another big-ticket item, you may not get a favorable interest rate, causing you to pay a higher monthly payment, while eroding your ability to save.

On the other hand, if you studied to be a doctor, a corporate attorney, an IT specialist, or a registered nurse, your income after graduation will be much higher, giving you a lower DTI Ratio. (Allowing you to qualify for an FHA mortgage, so that you can purchase a house and start building wealth.) You will also be able to chip away at that Student Loan debt at a much faster pace.

So, why did the university or the financial institution allow you to take on that student loan debt, to become a School Teacher or a Social Worker? Knowing full well the predicament that you will be faced with? <u>It's a</u> **SCAM**!

The financial institution pays the university and a part of that money is added to the university's billion-dollar endowment. The financial institution makes money from the interest they charge you, and worst yet, that money is guaranteed by the government, payable with your tax dollars.

If a corporation borrowed that same $37,172 to start a different business, or took out a bridge loan for an existing business, and the economy went south, that corporation can file bankruptcy to discharge themselves of that debt, and in some cases start all over again.

You can file bankruptcy on student loan debt claiming undue hardship, but it's a very difficult process. Before taking on student loan debt, everyone should thoroughly evaluate the consequences. Please don't fall for the Student Loan **SCAM**!

Chapter 6

Use Stock Market Gains to Build Wealth

Some folks are afraid to invest in the stock market: (a) because of the risk involved and (b) because they've never taken the time to learn the basics of investing in the stock market.

Companies raise money to start businesses, grow and expand those businesses, or diversify their existing businesses. They raise cash by issuing Stock certificates, which can be converted to cash. If the company is publicly held, those certificates can be purchased or sold by the public (via a stock broker), on one of the following exchanges:

(1) The New York Stock Exchange

(2) The NASDAQ Exchange

(3) American Stock Exchange

(4) The Chicago Stock Exchange

(5) The Boston Stock Exchange

As the company's profits grow and as the public continue to purchase shares of the company stock, those Stock certificates become more valuable, and the price of the stock typically increases.

The reverse of that situation also applies. As the company loses money and generate losses, and as stockholders sell their shares, those stock certificates become less valuable and the price declines.

22

Municipalities like schools, courts, and police stations raise money by issuing municipal bonds. Public investors can purchase those bonds, and receive an annual interest payment (coupon), each year that they own the bond. The rate of returns on bonds are typically lower than that of stocks.

Over the long term, stocks do better. Since 1926, large stocks have returned an average of 10% per year. Long-term government bonds have returned between 5% and 6%, according to the investment researcher, Morningstar.[11]

Risk: You can lose money if you purchase stocks and the price declines.

Example: If you purchased 100 shares of stock @ $60/share = $6,000 and you sold your 100 shares for $50/share = $5,000 you've lost -$1,000.

If you Purchase Bonds and sell them before the maturity date for less than you paid, or if the issuer defaults on their payments, you can also **lose money.**

Municipal Bonds are safer investments, and they're a good fit for older investors who don't have the same amount of time that younger investors may have to recoup losses. Municipal bonds are less risky because most of them are GO (General Obligation) bonds. If for some reason that bond is in jeopardy of default, the bond issuer has an obligation to secure it with taxpayers dollars.

Reward:

Example #1:

On the other hand, if on January 1, 2019 you purchased 100 shares of a NASDAQ traded stock for $60/share (60 x 100 = $6,000) and on December 31, 2019 your stock, like the average NASDAQ stock in 2019, gained 37.89%, and you sold the 100 shares for $82.74/share = $8,274, you would have gained $2,274.00

Example #2: On January 1, 2019 had you invested your $6,000 in a short-term (1year) **Municipal Bond**, with an average annual 2019 YTD return of 6.91%. At the end of the year, December, 31 2019 your bond would be worth $6,312.71. You would have gained $321.71

Example #3: On January 1, 2019 had you placed your $6,000 in a **Bank Savings Account**, your $6,000 with the average 2019 YTD return of 1.5% would have grown to $6,090.62 on December 31, 2019. You would have gained a whopping $90.62.

Question? If you receive $900/month rent from your rental property, and after paying your $300/month mortgage, $65/month taxes, $19/month insurance, and $16/month maintenance you're left with a profit of $500/month x 12 months = $6,000/year, *how will you invest your $6,000?*

1. Will you invest it in the Stock Market and make a potential $2,274?
2. Will you invest it in a Municipal Bond and make a potential $321.71?
3. Will you place it in a Bank Savings Account and make $90.62? Or
4. Will you place it "Under Your Mattress and make $0"!

Investing in the stock market has risks and rewards. Like anything else, educating yourself on the stock market will help you reduce risk, and allow you to be more comfortable as you seek greater returns on your investments.

Doing Research: Which stocks should I purchase?
Start your research by first selecting a brokerage firm with an online research portal that you're comfortable with. I use Charles Schwab's. It's very user friendly and I can track stocks before buying them by putting them on a Schwab watchlist (which I create myself.)
Next open a **Roth IRA** and a regular **trading account** at the brokerage firm you select. You're doing this for several reasons. (a) You're saving some cash for your retirement which you'll

be funding with after tax dollars, so that when you retire you can withdraw your money tax free. (b) If you need cash for an emergency, you can tap into it and avoid some of the penalties you would have incurred with a traditional IRA. You can deposit $6,000 every year, or $7,000 (If you're 50 and older) into your Roth IRA. The other brokerage account, will be used to park your cash after you've funded your IRA. Historically, if you invest those funds by purchasing stocks, your returns will be much higher than if you place your money in a bank savings account.

All research portals, have a section that display **Stock Sectors** and they rank those sectors (or industries) based on returns (1 Day/30 Days/1 Year.) Here's a list of Sectors on Schwab's Portal ranked (1Year – June 3, 2020)

Information Technology	**+36.53%**
Health Care	**+18.74%**
Consumer Discretionary	**+14.39%**
Consumer Staples	+7.19%
Materials	+6.39%
Utilities	+2.62%
Communication Services	- 2.45%
Industrials	-3,73%
Real Estate	-6.44%
Financials	-9.45%
Energy	-31.16%

I normally pick stocks from the **3 hottest Sectors.** From the example above, I would select my stocks from: Info Tech/ Health Care & Consumer Discretionary. **Drilling down further, you can select stocks with:**

1. The biggest % price Increase Ytd

2. The biggest % price Decrease Ytd

3. Stocks with the biggest $ price Increase Ytd

4. Stocks with the biggest $ price Decrease Ytd

5. Stocks with 52 Week Highs

6. Stocks with 52 Week Lows

7. Or the Most Active stocks in a sector.

If you select the top 3 sectors showing the biggest $ Price gains Ytd, or the most active stocks of those top 3 sectors Ytd, Schwab will actually list those stocks for you.

Which Stocks Do I Pick? And What's My Buying Criteria?

1. My stock has to be **Under $50/share**. (I can buy more shares when the price is low.)

2. My stock has to be **outperforming the 3 major indexes:** The S&P 500, the Dow, and the Nasdaq, by at least 25% Points Ytd. Example: If the leading Index is Up an average of 40% Ytd, my stock has to be Up by 65+% Ytd.

3. My stock has to be **trending upwards**. (I place the stock's performance on a mountain graph and view the performance over the past 12 months)

4. Good Fundamentals: the company has to be well financed, with no pending litigation, and no dumping by the officers. If the company is in the midst of a major lawsuit, they could lose and be forced to pay out billions, which could force stockholders to sell, thus reducing the value of the stock. If officers are reducing ownership and selling their shares in large quantities, that's suspicious. They could be taking gains (which is ok). However, they may be acting on negative inside information and may be dumping.

5. If my stocks meet **ALL 4 Criteria – It's A BUY!** (If it meets 3 of 4) I place it on a watchlist and monitor the performance.

Using a Watchlist to Track Stocks:

Most brokerage portals will allow you to place stocks on a watchlist so that you can track the performance before you purchase the stock. You can create a mountain graph to track the stock's upward growth. You can also compare the performance of that stock, to the performance of the 3 major indexes:

1) **The S&P 500** - The 500 largest U.S. stocks by market capitalization.
2) **The Dow Jones Industrials** – 30 companies that cover all of the major sectors except for Transportation and Utilities.
3) **The NASDAQ Composite** – 3,300 companies the majority of which are in the Information Technology sector.

After being placed on a watchlist, if my stock starts to trend upward and finally **meets all 4 criteria**, I again check recent articles on the company to make sure that there's no **negative publicity** or **pending litigation** surrounding the company.

I also check to see whether **officers are dumping**, and whether there are any **large accounting write-offs.** If all is well, then I go ahead and **Pull the Trigger** and purchase that stock.

<u>Monitoring Stocks I've Purchased</u>:
Like my checking accounts, I check my stocks every day. It only takes a few minutes, and after all it's my hard-earned money. If a stock is trending downward I'm not going to panic and sell without giving it some time. After one quarter (3 months) of showing a downward trend, I check the sector to see if the economy has negatively affected that sector. If the sector has not been negatively affected by the economy, I dig a little deeper to determine whether the company had any recent accounting write-offs, negative publicity, or unfavorable litigation.

If the downward trend reaches the point where it's no longer outperforming the (S&P 500, the Dow and the Nasdaq) by 25+%, then it's time to sell that stock and replace it with one from my watchlist that meets my buying criteria. I never fall in love with a stock that's under performing. An underperforming stock is tying up my money that could be giving me a nice return on my investment.

Purchasing Gold as a Hedge for Inflation

Many investors purchase gold, as a hedge for inflation. You can purchase physical gold coins, or you can purchase ETFs (Exchange Traded Funds) – Stocks that invest in gold miners.

Risky Trading:
Buying on Margin/ Short Selling/Crypto Trading

I avoid risky trading, for the simple fact that I've been able to make a nice return on my investments by doing my own research, sticking to my buying and selling criteria, and by buying *Long*.

Buying Stocks on Margin:

Buying stocks on margin involves borrowing money from a broker to purchase stocks. A margin account increases your purchasing power, and allows you to use someone else's money to increase your financial leverage. However, there's a cost associated with borrowing money. It's called *interest*! If your stock drastically declines in price, and there's a margin call by the financial institution, you can potentially lose more money than you initially invested. You can lose your initial investment plus the interest you were charged when you borrowed that money.

Short Selling:

Short selling or "shorting" is a risky method of investing. Investors expect the stock to lose value, so they borrow stocks and immediately sell them in hopes of making a profit.

Example: If XYZ stock is trading at $100/share and you borrow 50 Shares and immediately sell them, that transaction cost you $5,000. If XYZ stock drops to $50 per share, and you return the 50 shares Paying $2,500 you've just made a nice $2,500 Profit. However, if XYZ stock value increases to $150 per share, and you return the 50 shares, at $7,500 – You will lose $2,500.

Investing in Bitcoin and other Cryptocurrencies:

Unlike other currencies, "crypto," the virtual currency is decentralized and not backed by any government or central bank. Instead, it relies on cryptography (special codes) to make it secure, and a virtual public ledger known as "blockchain" to keep track of transactions and make it difficult to hack or counterfeit.

Crypto is the virtual currency, and blockchain technology is the accounting system for tracking crypto transactions. Each transaction is considered a block, and several blocks create a chain. You can invest in both the virtual currencies (crypto) or you can invest in the accounting technology that track them (blockchain technology).

Bitcoin the (first crypto) was created in 2009, and is one of thousands of digital currencies out there. Like gold, crypto is an alternative for investors seeking a hedge for inflation. It's not vulnerable to inflation like the US dollar. In that regard it's safe, but is it dangerous? Bitcoin has somewhat of a shady past being linked to the Silk Road (Dark Web[12]) website, where money laundering, funding illegal drugs and weapon sales took place. But now several legit companies like Overstock and PayPal accept Bitcoin. Although crypto has gone mainstream, hackers and people involved in nefarious activities prefer to be paid in crypto to avoid being exposed. The Danger and volatility of crypto, can also be attributed to the "Pump & Dump Schemes" which often take place, due to the lack of regulation within this new industry. An individual or a group of people who plan to make a quick profit first **pump** an asset into the market by purchasing a large quantity of coins, pushing the demand and price of the respective coin upward. Then, they quickly **dump** (sell) and release the assets at a higher price, to rake in a quick return on the investment.

What about the carbon footprint? The amount of electricity and energy needed to encrypt and verify blockchain transactions is huge. Those supercomputers use so much electricity, that Elon Musk says Tesla will no longer accept Bitcoin. As you can see, crypto is relatively new, somewhat unregulated, and its volatility makes it much riskier than stocks and bonds. Just like stocks, crypto is bought and sold on exchanges; you can also track prices and view charts and market capitalizations on websites like **CoinMarketCap.com**.

In summary, "Crypto" is virtual currency. You can put physical cash in your wallet or deposit it in your physical bank. However, when you purchase crypto currency, you get a set of keys consisting of (several numbers letters and characters) which are randomly produced by supercomputers using complicated math formulas called algorithms. That process is called "mining". Those KEYS, produced by mining are your passwords used to access your virtual coins on the internet. You can exchange, swap, or sell your virtual coins on the internet. Those transactions are recorded in a **new** virtual accounting system called "Blockchain Technology".

Pros:

There's **no government control** of Crypto yet! But legislation is currently being written in Congress, to Tax Crypto very soon.

Privacy: You can conduct financial transactions with a high degree of privacy.

Inflation Proof: Like gold, Crypto is a good hedge for inflation.

Cons:

Hackers: Although mining can create an extremely high level of security, hackers have shown the ability to unlock those codes and steal Crypto coins. The Internet infrastructure company PolyNetwork was recently hacked for $600M.

Lost or Stolen Keys: If you lose or forget your keys, or if your computer hard-drive crashes, or if someone steals your computer and takes your keys from the hard-drive, you can lose millions. The FBI can't really help you and the FDIC **will not** insure your Crypto coins, allowing you to recover the maximum $250,000. (So, You're Basically Screwed!)

As more mainstream companies accept cryptocurrency, and as blockchain technology improves, perhaps Crypto's volatility will subside thereby reducing the risk associated with it.   But, as of now it remains a risky investment.

Why should you Invest in the Stock Market?

Over the past three years, the stock market has been literally "Kicking Ass"!!!

Especially Nasdaq traded stocks, which include several technology companies.

COVID-19 presented a hiccup, however if you had the foresight to invest in companies involved in making COVID vaccines, then any losses you incurred could have been offset by those Vaccine Stock gains. I purchased one of those stocks at $33/Share, and it's now trading over $262/Share. At one point during this year, it went up to $464/Share. I purchased another one at $32/Share, and it's now trading at $254/Share. At one point this year, it went up to $497/Share.

Consider the Following Returns:

(www.slickcharts.com)	2019	2020	2021
Nasdaq:	37.96%	47.58%	20.04%
S&P 500	31.49	18.40	25.51
DOW	22.34	7.25	15.96

My Investment Goal is to outperform the "Best of the Best Above, by 25% to 50% Every Year"!

At the end of the past 3 years, me and several Investors have consistently ended the year "Way above those numbers". And I'm no Genius!

Of all of the Rental Properties I purchase over the past 3 years, my 20% Down Payment, came from my "Stock Market Gains". So, I was basically building my wealth, with "House Money". (Now That's a Beautiful Thing!). If you're not comfortable selecting your own Stocks, then please hook up with a Stock-Broker who can help you. Two Heads coming together, is better than one. I would start by looking at Edward Jones. Why?

1) The Company is Headquartered right here in St. Louis MO – My Backyard, and I know some of their Brokers and Partners.

2) The Company seems to be committed to "Diversity & Inclusion".

3) They have Black Brokers, and some of their Partners are Black. They seem to be talking the talk while walking the walk.

I would call them, and ask them to recommend one of their "Black Brokers" to help you. Why Black? (Just in case you forgot – The Title of this Book is "Building Black Wealth.")

Chapter 7

Consider a Career or Investments that pays Residual Income

<u>Residual income</u> is income you receive every month after the work is done. Residual income is paid to you, with little or no effort on your part, after completing the sale, or after completing the job.

Some careers that offer residual income are: life insurance agents/brokers, health insurance agents/brokers, home and auto insurance agents, authors, movie makers, and ATM owners. Whenever you pay your insurance premium, your agent or broker receives a small portion of your monthly premium payment. A health insurance broker selling Medicare Advantage Plans, receives $24/month per client after the first year, as long as that client keeps his or her Medicare Advantage Plan. If that broker has 300 clients, that's $7,200/month residual income (every freaking month without having to do anything.)

Consider a career in filmmaking or writing. You can **Make a Movie** or **Publish a Book** and receive residual income whenever someone watches your movie or purchases your book.

Investments that Pay Residual Income:

Real estate is an example of an investment that pays residual income. You can rent your house or a room or an apartment for a week or a weekend, and receive residual income. You can use the property as an Airbnb property and also receive residual income. Real estate can also give you passive income, if you have someone renting your property (permanently.)

Dividend Stocks that pay regular dividends is another source of residual income.

Owning an ATM will give you residual income whenever someone uses your ATM. Those $3, $4 or $5 ATM fees you collect, depending on where your ATM is located, can be a nice source of residual income. The beautiful thing about Residual Income is the fact that after the work is done, it requires little or no effort on your part, and you constantly receive that income. Career changes are sometimes difficult for some folks to undertake. Some individuals simply do not like sales. If your personality makes it difficult for you to engage in sales, or if you're a reclusive individual then you can write a book or purchase dividend paying stocks as a means of receiving some residual income.

Another beautiful thing about residual income, is the fact that it can supplement your retirement income. Some folks retire without a pension and have to rely strictly on their social security income. Very few companies offer their employees pensions today. If you did not fund a 401K, or if your company does not pay a pension, having some residual income to supplement your social security will no doubt enhance your retirement, and eliminate lots of financial stress.

Chapter 8

How will a Natural Disaster like COVID-19 Affect Your Wealth?

As I write this short chapter, our nation is confronted with the COVID-19 virus, a pandemic of unprecedented proportions. Thousands of Americans have gotten ill and many have lost their jobs. If you lose your job, are you able to:

(a) Pay your rent or your mortgage?

(b) Pay your credit card bills?

(c) Pay your utilities?

(d) Purchase food?

(e) Save cash?

(f) Invest in real-estate or foreclosures that will flood the market?

The consequences of not paying your rent, your mortgage, or your bills on time can be catastrophic, even though it's no fault of yours. This situation can lead to foreclosures, poor credit ratings, poor FICO scores, and several years of sitting on the sidelines struggling, while you're unable to build wealth.

COVID-19 caused 42 million Americans to be unemployed, and millions never regained their jobs. Several folks were forced to file bankruptcy, and foreclosed on their homes, as the level of economic uncertainty became astounding.

What if your company files for bankruptcy and you lose your job? What if your Unemployment runs out? What if you lose your health insurance (which is tied to your job) and you become sick? What if you're unable to find a job in your field? What if you exhaust your emergency fund, and you have no cash to cover your living expenses?

The stress associated with the above situations can affect your health and compound matters even more. Statistics show that the number one cause of bankruptcy, is the inability to pay medical bills.

As you can see, a pandemic or a natural disaster can have a profound effect on our ability to survive. Not only can it affect our day to day lives, but it can definitely limit our ability to build wealth. All of which leads to our next topic of discussion: **Jobs** vs. **Trades and Self-Employment!**

Chapter 9

Jobs vs. Trades and Self Employment

If you were one of the unfortunate individuals who lost their job, health insurance, home (due to foreclosure), and have exhausted all of your emergency funds as a result of COVID-19 (at no fault of your own), perhaps now is the time to evaluate the predicament you've placed yourself in by having a job, instead of possessing skills from a TRADE! Perhaps now is the time to consider Self Employment. To consider generating Residual Income and Passive Income. To review your annual income, your time, your quality of your life, and your overall *destiny*!

It's not too late to salvage your life. Depending on your age, you can pick up the pieces, explore new opportunities, and acquire some new skills. If you like sales, get your health & life insurance licenses, and consider being self-employed.

Consider being self-employed in a field that gives you residual income and passive income. Having acquired the skills of a plumber, mason, carpenter, or hairdresser would allow you to receive income constantly, regardless of the economy. Depending on how resourceful you are, you and only you, will determine how much money you make. You will also have control over when and how many hours you work.

If you're an insurance broker who owns two rental properties with each paying a net of $500/month profit ($1,000 Total), while also receiving $24/month residual income on each of your 300 Medicare Advantage Clients ($7,200 total), that's **$8,200** passive and residual income you'll receive each month, while sitting at home like millions of other Americans awaiting the end of the pandemic. That's the beauty of passive income and residual income.

As you age and mature, you'll notice that **Time** is your greatest asset. You can spend your time working for yourself building your book of business that will give you residual income in perpetuity, or you can spend your time on a job building someone else's business and growing their wealth. *The choice is yours.*

If you're self-employed, you can take naps or play a round of golf in the middle of the day or you can take extended vacations whenever you please, see the world, and check things off of your bucket list! You control your wealth, your time and ultimately your destiny.

A very good friend of mine is a contractor, who builds and rehab houses. Regardless of the time of the year, or peaks and valleys of the economy, my friend is always busy. His plate is so full, that he is constantly turning down jobs due to lack of time, and due to a shortage of skilled laborers like himself.

Start today, evaluate your career choices. If you're unable to handle physical labor, then acquire the skills that will allow you to work with your pen. Seek help and ask questions. You'll be surprised to know how many people are willing to offer you free advice on various careers. If you own a home, start with your insurance agent, or your real estate broker.

Ask them questions about their careers. Find out if they have a contractor, plumber, mason, carpenter, or handyman to which they refer clients. Speak to those experts about how they acquired their skills. Consider learning a trade and becoming an apprentice. Use your social media (Facebook/ LinkedIn) to seek networking assistance. The Internet offers you an unlimited amount of resources from the comfort of your own home. Use your resources to help you with your career change.

Chapter 10

Protect your Assets and Build Generational Wealth with Life Insurance

There are three types of life insurance that are commonly used today. There's **Whole Life Insurance**, which is primarily used to bury you or to cover your final expenses. There's **Term Insurance**, which is used to protect your assets and build generational wealth. Lastly, **Universal Life Insurance** is an Insurance product with an investment component. I don't like using insurance as an investment because the returns are minimal, so we'll be discussing two of the three (whole life insurance and term insurance.)

One constant in life, is the fact that at some point we all will die and we will have to be buried. Whole Life Insurance was designed for one purpose, and that purpose is to bury you. That's why whole life insurance is often referred to as **final expense insurance.**

The average cost of a funeral today is approximately $10,000. The beauty of whole life insurance is the fact that once you purchase that policy, your premiums never change regardless of your age or health.

One constant in the life insurance industry, is the fact that the younger you are, and the healthier you are, the less money you will pay for your coverage. The insurance actuaries have figured out that young healthy people, live longer than old sick people. Thus, **less risk = lower cost!**
Knowing the above information, and the fact that we will all have

to be buried at some point, we should purchase that $10,000 Policy ASAP, because the cost increases with age.

Whole Life Insurance Quotes: ($10,000 Coverage)

As a Child Rider - Age 15 Days to 18 Years - **$2.09/Month**

At age 19 Male - $16.24/Month

At age 19 Female - $14.96/Month

At age 40 Male - $23.10/Month

At age 40 Female - $20.10/Month

At age 65 Male - $57.94/Month

At age 65 Female - $43.85/Month

Age 70 Male - *Unhealthy - $119.58/Month

Age 70 Female - *Unhealthy - $102.08/Month

(These are healthy non-tobacco quotes with guaranteed issuing and unhealthy quotes, meaning previous stroke, heart attack, cancer, and/or dementia, with a 2-year waiting period, from two reputable life insurance companies.) Whole Life payments never change. Payments are the same your <u>whole life</u>!

Term Insurance gives you more coverage for your money, however the coverage is for a term: 10, 20, or 30 years. When that 10, 20, or 30 years is up, the policy ends and you have no more insurance coverage.

Term Insurance is used to protect your assets while building generational wealth. If a young couple each 30 years of age, purchase their first home for $400,000 with a 30 Year mortgage, they can each purchase a $500,000 (30 Year Term Life Insurance Policy) to protect that house (their biggest asset.) The monthly premiums (from a reputable insurance company) on the male policy will be $33.44/month, and for the female $28.16/month, with premiums totaling $61.60/month. Since the mortgage is for 30 years, the 30 year term policy will protect them throughout the entire repayment period of their 30-year mortgage loan.

In the event that one spouse should die, without that $500,000 term insurance policy (which can be used to pay off the $400,000 Mortgage) it will be very difficult for the remaining spouse to pay that $2,500 Monthly Mortgage payment, along with all of the other living expenses, including the children's school or college tuition.

Eventually, foreclosure procedures could kick in causing the remaining spouse to lose the house. For $61.60/month, the couple could have protected that $400,000 investment, which gained equity over the years. The remaining spouse could have also pocketed $100,000 to cover future expenses or the children's college tuition.

Please Note: During the 30 years of ownership of the house that was purchased for $400,000, with appreciating home values, that home could now be worth over $1,000,000. Term Insurance, gave that couple 1,000,000 reasons, to protect their biggest investment for "Only $61.60 a month".

In summary, whole life insurance should be used primarily to bury you as your final expense. Term insurance is used to protect your assets (home and/or business) and it could also be used to create a legacy to be passed on to your children and your grandchildren (generational wealth) in the event that the insured passes.

If you have no insurance and no savings when you die, while still grieving for you, your family will have to pass the hat or create a Go Fund Me in order to collect that $10,000 to bury you.

Please don't put your family in that predicament. Buy your $10K whole life policy **today!** It's your obligation. It's your *final* expense. If you have a Home Mortgage, or a Business, protect your investment. Purchase a 30 year Term Policy, to pay off your mortgage or other business debt, should you pass before the 30 years.

Chapter 11

Using Reverse Mortgages To Enjoy Life & Pass on Wealth

In chapter 4, we discussed using reverse mortgages as a way of avoiding foreclosure. In this chapter, we'll discuss using reverse mortgages as a way to enjoy your life <u>right now</u> and leave a legacy for your loved ones. Some of us who were not fortunate to retire with a pension, and who have very little savings, may be currently struggling to make ends meet while living primarily on Social Security Income. Despite your financial situation, you may still want to leave a legacy for your children and your grandchildren.

If you own a home, you can acquire a reverse mortgage, continue to live in your home, and leave a nice legacy for your loved ones. A **Reverse Mortgage** is a loan based on the equity in your home. It's also based on your age. The older you are and the more equity you have in your home, the more money you can pull out. **Requirements:** Home Equity Conversion Mortgages (HECMs), the most common type of reverse mortgage loans, require that the homeowners must be 62 years of age or older. Your home must be your principal residence (where you live the majority of the year.) You can either own your home outright, or have a remaining mortgage balance. Some lenders may require that you have at least 45% equity in your home. You can use your own funds, or proceeds from the reverse mortgage to pay off your existing mortgage balance.

You may not be delinquent on any federal debt, such as income taxes, or federal student loans. However, you may use funds from the reverse mortgage to pay off this debt. You must continue paying your property taxes, your insurance on the property, as well as maintenance and upkeep.

The house must be in good shape, or the lender may require that you make certain repairs, before giving you the loan. You must also receive counseling from HUD to discuss your eligibility, and the financial implications of the loan.

Please Note: When you do a reverse mortgage, the government **does not own your home.** Contrary to popular belief; you still own your home. You've simply taken out a loan on your home, which is due after you pass. If married, the loan is due after you both pass.

Since you don't make any monthly payments on a reverse mortgage, proof of your income, and /or high credit scores **are not** required. A credit check or a public records check, will only be used to confirm if you have any federal tax liens, or other items that may affect your qualification.

Like all loans, a reverse mortgage **has to be paid back**, however, the loan is **not due until after you die**. Whomever you willed your house to, or whomever you added to the title, has three options regarding repayment of the loan.

Option #1: They can give up the house, and walk away with no obligation.
Option #2: They can pay off the loan, and own the house outright.
Option #3: They can keep the house, assume the mortgage and make monthly mortgage payments.

The best way to do a reverse mortgage is to back it up with a term life insurance policy, as well as an interest-bearing investment product like a tax-free municipal bond. The interest on your municipal bond (6.91% - 2019 average) should be enough to pay the monthly premiums on the term life insurance policy, plus provide you with additional income.

Here's an example from a reputable insurance company:

You're a 70-year old female, your house was appraised at $150,000. You own the house outright (no mortgage balance.) You may be able to pull **$100,000** out via a reverse mortgage.

   (a) You can purchase a 15-year $125,000 term life insurance policy with a monthly premium of $124.74/month = **$1,496.88/year**

   (b) You can also purchase a $75,000 tax-free municipal bond, with an annual coupon payment of 6.91% **($5,182.50/ year.)** This will pay the above insurance premiums of $1,496.88, and provide you with $3,685.62 in additional income. At maturity, simply purchase another $75K bond.

   (c) You can also use **$25,000** from the proceeds of your reverse mortgage to treat yourself with a nice used car, or splurge a little and go on a cruise, or do both.

If you die at or before 85, your beneficiary will have $125,000 from the term life insurance policy, which can be used to pay off the ($100,000+ interest) reverse mortgage, and own your home outright. Plus, they will also have the $75,000 Municipal Bond, plus the coupon interest on that bond. If you outlive the term policy (85+), you can save the term premiums ($1,496.88/year), and pass those savings along with the $75,000 bond on to your beneficiary. Then, they can use it to pay off the reverse mortgage if they choose to. Note: To be compliant do not use cash from the proceeds of you reverse mortgage to pay your insurance premiums. Use your other cash.

To summarize, a reverse mortgage can be used to avoid foreclosure, or it can be used to splurge a little and enjoy some of your hard-earned equity "right now", while continuing to live in your home. If done correctly, it will allow you to leave a nice legacy for your loved ones, thereby contributing to your generational wealth.

Chapter 12

Reclaiming Your Parents or Your Grandparents Land

Reclaiming your parents or your grandparents land can be a challenging process. In addition to a host of family opinions questioning your audacity and your integrity, you will also have to deal with employees at the local county land records department, where good customer service can vary tremendously, and in some instances may not exist at all.

Some of your family members, although they're doing absolutely nothing to reclaim the family land, may be jealous of you for doing so. Some may not want to pitch in to help you pay the property taxes, but yet may demand their share of the proceeds from the sale of the land. Some may question your integrity and accuse you of stealing their inheritance, although they themselves are doing nothing to take back the property. In addition to securing the correct property address and parcel number, you will need <u>the legal description of the property</u>, and you <u>may</u> or <u>may not</u> need:

- A warranty deed
- A quit claim deed
- A grant deed
- A contract for deed
- A property agreement
- An affidavit of title - Or
- A host of other legal documents

Depending on whether your parents or grandparents are still alive, and are able to sign legal documents. You will need to know the current tax status of the land, and whether or not it has a clean title, or if it has any outstanding liens? Your parents and grandparents may have died with or without having a will, so you may also have some probate issues.

In order to reduce the stress affiliated with all of the above, I suggest that you first gather all of the documents you can get your hands on, like: wills, titles, pictures of the land, tax records, tax receipts, deeds or any documents relating to the land. Then, go to the county office in charge of land records, and gather as much information on the land that you possibly can. They can give you the lot # and the deed showing ownership or Transfer of Ownership, as well as a statement showing any outstanding taxes on the property.

You can then head to the Mayor's office or the City Manager's office, and get a copy of the10-year plan for the area that your land sits on, as well as the surrounding area. If they're plans to develop your land or land surrounding yours, you may want to pay the taxes, and wait until the developers present you with an offer. You may also consider developing that land yourself. In any event, it's good to know the future plans, because they will no doubt increase your options.

With all of the information you've gathered, you should then seek the assistance of a probate attorney to determine whether or not it's worth pursuing. You need to know all costs and legal fees involved in legally reclaiming your land.

Once you've properly secured title to you parents or your grandparents land, you now have the option of (a) selling it and securing a nice profit, or (b) passing it on to your loved ones via a **Quitclaim deed**, or (c) Placing it in a Trust with instructions to the trustee on paying the taxes, insurance, and upkeep, as well as instructions on future distribution of the property.

Chapter 13

Start a Business (Blacks need more Businesses)

With a population of 47.8 Million, and a buying power approaching $1.4 trillion it's time for Blacks in America to **own more** businesses. For those of you who may not be into numbers, this is what $1.4 trillion looks like: **$1,400,000,000,000.**

That's a whole lot of zeros and a whole lot of money, which we spend every freaking year with people **who don't look like us!** That's more money than the GDP (Gross Domestic Product) of several advanced nations! Going back to my college days when I majored in economics, I recalled that GDP was measured by adding up all the money spent by consumers, businesses, and the government in the period of a year. It may also be measured by adding up all of the money received by all the participants in the economy during that year. Please consider this:

The GDP of **Canada** was $1.736 trillion in 2019
The GDP of **Russia** was $1.7 trillion in 2019
The GDP of **Mexico** was $1.269 trillion in 2019
The GDP of **Ireland** was $388.7 billion in 2019
The GDP of **South Africa** was $351.4 billion in 2019
The GDP of **Jamaica** was $16.46 billion in 2019

Blacks in America spend **$1.4 trillion** every year, and those dollars stay in the Black community for just **6 Hours!** Contrarily, Asian dollars circulate within the Asian community for 28 days, Jewish dollars circulate within the Jewish community for 19 days, and White dollars circulate within the white community for 17 days. In economics, there's a term for Blacks spending our money outside of our community and giving our hard-earned money to people who don't look like us; it's called **"Economic Leakage"**.

If Blacks spent <u>only 5% of our $1.4 trillion</u> with Black businesses within the Black community and keep circulating those Black dollars, that would give a tremendous boost to Black businesses, allowing them to expand and diversify.

The ripple effects would also be significant. Blacks can now hire other Blacks and offer good wages, lower Black unemployment and foster entrepreneurship that ultimately leads to the creation of "Generational Black Wealth". We can pass those businesses on to our families – for generations!

In the book *"Our Black Year"* by Maggie and John Anderson[13], the authors conducted an experiment, whereby the couple and their two small daughters would try to live for one year completely purchasing all of their food, clothing, and household supplies from Black-owned businesses in Chicago. In a major city like Chicago, conducting the experiment was a struggle. There simply weren't enough black-owned businesses in this major city, to accommodate the Andersons.

Blacks in America cannot reduce economic leakage unless we create businesses to capture that $1.4 trillion dollars. It's a very simple concept. We create businesses, we support those businesses, and we circulate $1.4 trillion within our communities. We've done it before, back in the 1920's with **Black Wall Street**[14].

We developed thriving African American communities in Tulsa, Oklahoma and Durham, North Carolina. Blacks in those communities owned barber shops, hair salons, grocery stores, movie theaters, doctor's offices, dental offices, schools, churches, restaurants, pool halls and bowling alleys. Black dollars were circulated and stayed in those Black communities **over 36 Days.** As a result, there was little economic leakage, and a thriving Black middle class developed. We were actually **"Building Black wealth!"**

We've done it before, and we certainly can do it again, especially now that the stakes are so high - **$1.4 trillion dollars.**

Chapter 14

Estate Planning
(Trusts, Wills, Deeds, TODs, & Beneficiary Assignments)

We're not going to be around forever, so we should all have a plan "clearly defining" how we want to pass our assets and our wealth on to our loved ones. Without a "Clearly Defined Plan", **there will be**: difficulties, mistrust, anxiety, confusion, stress, and lots of "Unnecessary Added Expenses".In order to eliminate this experience after we pass, and in order to avoid having the State make those decisions for us through probate, we should all have an estate plan with clear and concise instructions on how to distribute our assets after we die.

Please take the time to read and understand the purpose of the following documents: trusts, wills, deeds, TODs, beneficiary assignments. Please hire a professional to help you select the one that's right for you. A good financial planner can review all of your assets, and based on the laws in your state, tell you whether or not you need a Trust, a simple Will, TODs, or beneficiary assignments, in order to transfer your assets upon death.

If you own real-estate, there's a good chance that your estate will have to be probated after you pass. So, you will probably need to set up a trust, in order to avoid the time and expense of going through the probate process. Please don't try to play attorney and do it yourself. I tried playing Attorney twice in my lifetime and both outcomes were disastrous.

When I was a youngster, I had an issue with a credit card company that ended in court. At the time, I was struggling financially and decided to play attorney and represent myself. The credit card company was well represented with two attorneys. When the judge asked me about filing a motion, I didn't have a clue about what she was talking about! I almost wound up getting a judgement.

Later on in life, I decided again to play attorney and create a living will for my aging parents. It was a good thought, however I didn't take the time to research the laws in the state of New York regarding real-estate. I thought that by simply having a will, me and my siblings could avoid probate. NOT! After both my parents passed, we had to probate their estate. It was a long, daunting, and expensive process, which created lots of stress and anxiety among my siblings and I.

Please know your limitations. If you're a plumber, carpenter, car dealer or an insurance broker, please *do that*; stay in your lane and leave the legal stuff to the attorneys. Depending on the amount of assets you possess, instructions to pass them on after your death, can be documented in a simple Will or a TOD (Transfer on Death) deed. TOD's can be used for checking accounts, savings accounts, or vehicles you own. Some states will allow you to do a TOD on Real-Estate, allowing you to avoid probate. Some will not. So, if you or your loved one's own real-estate, and want to pass it on the correct way, please research the laws of your state, or the state of your loved ones.

Beneficiary Assignments are required for pensions, 401Ks, securities like stocks and bonds, life insurance, and health savings accounts, in order to pass those funds on to your loved ones. So, if you own any of those, please make sure that your beneficiary assignments are "accurate and up to date".

Quitclaim deeds transfer or add property ownership. They can only be used to avoid probate, if they are signed prior to the Grantor's death. Quitclaim deeds are commonly used by family

51

members to transfer ownership rights, or in divorces to transfer ownership in property between divorcing spouses. A quitclaim deed makes no promises about **the grantor having a clear title**. It simply transfers ownership rights the grantor has, with no guarantees.

Warranty deeds are legal documents, that are commonly used in Real-estate transactions to transfer ownership, with the grantor guaranteeing that the property has no liens. About half of the states in the U.S. will permit a property owner to transfer real estate with a TOD Deed (Transfer-On-Death Deed). The decedent must have recorded the deed before their death, in the county where the property is located, before the beneficiary can take title of the property. This can be done without the assistance of an executor, thereby avoiding probate.

Joint Ownership of Property is probably the best way to avoid probate. It doesn't matter if you're married or not. If the property is designated as a jointly held property, it's going to go to the surviving member or members, thereby avoiding probate.

A **Living Trust** is merely an alternative to a last will. Unlike a will, which merely distributes your assets upon death, a living trust places your assets and property in trusts, which are then managed by a trustee for the benefit of your beneficiaries.  It allows you to avoid probate entirely because the property and assets are already distributed to the trust.

Statistics on Probating an Estate are as follows: The average estate takes two years to probate. Court fees can range between 3 to 7 % of the value of the estate. The average amount spent on legal and accounting fees to settle an estate is approximately $11,400.

The Probate Process can sometimes be lengthy, and also very expensive. The executor of my parents' will, chose a probate attorney with which one of my siblings and I were uncomfortable. This guy was approaching 90 years of age and was grumpy as hell. When I asked him what it would cost to probate our parents' small estate, he was offended and wouldn't give me a straight answer. As I continued to question him, he had the audacity to hang up the phone on me.

Not only did his action piss me off, but it also created an enormous amount of friction between my siblings for three years. One of my siblings and I felt that we should seek the services of another probate attorney, the other two (one of who was the executor) wanted to keep him. The executor won that battle, which didn't sit well with the other two of us.

Dealing with Courts: In the middle of our probate process, the COVID-19 pandemic struck New York City extremely hard. As a result, all of the courts were closed. Dealing with courts during normal times is difficult. It takes forever to access information. Try dealing with courts during a pandemic! Needless to say, it added another year to our probate process. Our parents' estate was eventually settled after three years, with lots of stress and anxiety, and a price-tag that exceeded $11,400.

In summary, we should all take the time to correctly pass on our assets to our loved ones. That may require a simple will, TOD's, or beneficiary assignments. If you own real-estate, there's a good chance that it may require a trust in order to avoid probate. In any event, please take the time while you're healthy and of sound mind to do your research, in order to pass on your assets correctly.

Chapter 15

Succession Plans

If you own a business, at some point you may want to retire, or health issues may force you to cut back on the number of hours you work. Grooming a family member, or a loyal employee to take over after you step down, should be a goal of every business owner.

All of your sweat equity should not go down the drain, after you retire, or if you're forced to leave as a result of health issues. After all, you've worked extremely hard to build your business. All of the blood, sweat and tears you put into growing your business, should not be for naught.

One of the goals of every family business owner should be to pass his or her business on to the next generation, thus, securing generational wealth for his or her great-great-great grandchildren. A lot rides on planning a major transition within a company. Ensuring a smooth transition from one generation to the next is a process that needs to be carefully planned, and meticulously executed in order to succeed. It involves a lot of moving parts. If not done correctly, it can result in conflict, loss of assets and revenue, loss of good clients, and lots of damaged relationships. Some business relationships take a long time to foster. When I owned my car dealership, a gentleman came in every three months for an oil change. While my technicians were changing his oil, he made it a point to visit the showroom and pace back and forth in front of my office. One day I invited him in, to sit and chat, and he was delighted.

This gentleman once owned a family business and retired after passing it on to his children. Although he was worth millions, he drove the same old Crown Victoria with almost 200,000 miles on it. After a year of stopping in every three months to get his oil changed, one day he told me that I reminded him of himself when he started his business. He said that he wanted me to succeed, so he was going to introduce me to his brother, who ordered cars for a major rental car agency.

Shortly after this conversation, he brought his brother in and introduced him to me. The next day his brother came back, and ordered 200 cars from my dealership, for his rental car fleet.

That relationship took over 1 year to foster. This old guy simply wanted some attention (which I gave him) and he relished in the courtesy I extended to him. If my son, or daughter took over my car dealership, and didn't invite this old gentleman to sit in their office and shoot the breeze while getting his oil changed, there's a good chance that relationship (which took me a year to foster), would end abruptly, without them even knowing.

Ensuring a smooth transition from one generation to another takes time. It can be a slow lengthy process that needs to be carefully planned in order to ensure success.

If you have a family business, I strongly recommend getting all of your children involved at an early age. The earlier the better! Pre-teens are ideal. Give them chores to complete around your business and require that they help all of your employees in various departments, so that they can learn the business. And pay them! The sooner they develop a work ethic and the ability to manage money, the sooner they will develop to be responsible young adults, someone you can trust to take over the family business when you retire.

With careful grooming after several years, you will observe which family member or which loyal employee has the leadership skills, the business acumen, the sales skills, and the temperament to follow you as CEO. Sometimes that person may not be one of your children. It may be a loyal employee.

After several years of working for you, how do you explain to your children that an outsider or a loyal employee is more suited to run the company? Succession planning is not easy. There are companies out there that can help you with your transition. Being early and proactive about your family business succession planning will minimize conflict and maximize the ability for the business to do well in the future.

There are three main aspects of a family business transition:

1) Evaluating the interest and ability of the next generation, followed by grooming them for future leadership in your company is key. Figuring out the roles that suit them best, while instilling in them a sense of ownership is also important.

2) Working with the current generation to develop a plan that will enable them to step back enough to allow the next generation opportunities to develop themselves, and allow them to figure out what's next. Ensuring that harmony exists by preparing your entire family for cooperating with each other and respecting the designated leaders, is essential.

3) Figuring out which family members should get control versus ownership, and when they get that control is vital. Using the wrong process to reach decisions on leadership, wealth, and control, can create bigger issues within your family dynamic.

Having an outside consultant, not only takes that pressure off of you, but it ensures that the decisions you make are well thought out by professionals with experience in dealing with situations similar to yours. Finally, it's important to know and acknowledge that passing on a business to a family member isn't always a viable option for some business owners. You may have to develop a secondary plan to sell the business, or pass it on to a non-family member to ensure your family's wealth and peace of mind. Your son may have no interest in the family business at all. He may want to be a scientist or an astronaut. He may be the scientist who develops the cure for cancer. With the talent your son possesses, will society be best served with him toiling in your restaurant? Or in a laboratory doing his research? Your daughter may want to be a doctor or an attorney. You can't force them to take over your hardware store, or your restaurant, or your car dealership.

Sometimes, you may have to sell your business or pass it on to a non-family member. In conclusion, succession planning takes time, and it requires the assistance of Professionals in order *to get it right.*

Chapter 16

Paying Taxes to Uncle Sam

There's a Bible story in the book of Matthew where the Pharisees ask Jesus a tough question: "Tell us, is it against our law to pay taxes to Caesar or not?", (Matthew Chapter 22- Vs 15 -22.) Jesus responds, "Why are you trying to trap me? Show me the coin for paying the tax!" They brought him the coin and he asks them, "Whose face and name are these?" "Caesar's," they replied. Then Jesus said to them, "Give to Caesar what is Caesar's, and give to God what is Gods." Jesus was not against paying taxes, so why should we be?

I know you may be pissed off that the *very wealthy* avoid paying their fair share of taxes. They hire expensive lawyers and accountants to find loopholes in the tax codes. They invest in offshore projects to hide income, and they lobby politicians to change the inheritance tax laws. *I get that and I'm pissed too that they get away with it!* But let's not forget – There are several important reasons <u>why we should all pay taxes</u>:

1) How about building and maintaining the highways, roads and bridges that we use every day?
2) How about money to pay the teachers who teach our kids?
3) How about money to pay our police, firemen, and paramedics who take grandma to the hospital when she's having a heart attack?
4) How about money to pay the firemen who rescue us when we're trapped in our car, as a result of a bad car accident?
5) How about money to maintain our parks and recreation

facilities that enable us to enjoy a good quality of life!

6) How about the money to maintain our reservoirs, so that we can have clean drinking water. And, how about money to maintain our sewer systems, that prevent the spread of Diseases. *I Could Go on and on ....!*

We certainly don't want to overpay, but if we want to enjoy the quality of life that escapes "third world countries", then we all have to pay our taxes!

Filing Your Taxes:

Should you file them yourself, or should you hire a professional to file them for you? If you have a job and you receive a W2, and if you feel comfortable using Turbo-tax or another tax software product, then by all means file them yourself.

However, if you're self-employed and receive 1099's, or if you have a business, please have a professional prepare your taxes. Preferably a tax firm!

Tax firms have CPA's, MBA's, and some have Attorneys who can provide you with a variety of services, to ensure that your taxes are filed correctly and compliantly.

Unpaid Taxes:

If you have unpaid taxes, you will not be able to receive a mortgage or a business loan, thereby limiting your ability to build wealth. You may also be faced with garnishments. Tax liens are no longer included in credit reports, so they won't lower your credit scores. However, when you apply for a loan or other types of financing, the lenders may check your public records, and those tax liens could show up there. Those taxes will start accumulating penalties and interest! They're not going to mysteriously disappear, so you need to be proactive in formulating a plan of action to pay your taxes.

Where do you begin?

1) First it helps to know the exact amount of your debt, including the interest and penalties that you're dealing with. So, I would start by contacting the IRS and getting a current statement.

2) I would then contact a tax attorney and seek their assistance in developing a repayment plan.

3) You can also hire a tax relief company to negotiate on your behalf.

If you can't afford a tax attorney, or a tax relief company, then you can call the IRS and discuss an installment agreement, or the possibility of presenting them with an **<u>offer in compromise</u>**. Keep in mind, if you can't come to an agreement with the IRS, you have several appeals at your disposal. Exhaust them all! In any event, *pay your taxes* and keep it moving so that you can focus on building wealth. Taxes have been around since biblical times. They're a part of life. If you're self-employed or if you own a business, set aside enough money to pay your quarterly estimated taxes. Pay them throughout the year, so that you won't have sticker shock on April 15th.

Jesus said, "Give Caesar what's his." So, I'm saying to you, Give Uncle Sam what's his and keep it moving, so that you can focus on *building your wealth*!"

Chapter 17

Building Your Real-Estate Team

If you're a real-estate investor, it's critical that you have a good team of professionals to help you with the purchase and maintenance of your properties.

1. You have to purchase **good quality properties** to avoid spending lots of money on repairs down the road. You need a good inspector who will be honest with you, and point out flaws in your potential purchase. Having to replace a roof, or a sewer lateral could burn a hole in your pocket. So, check them thoroughly before you purchase that property. My Inspector Wes, has a keen eye in spotting potential flaws that could burn a hole in my pockets down the road.

2. You need a couple of **good real-estate agents** who are attuned to the market to help you find good locations and good homes that you can steal when you buy them. I have two - Robin Howard and Debbie Webber.

Remember when you purchase a home, you want to purchase at a low price. You want it to appreciate in value and you want to sell high so that you can make a nice profit. Your agents have to be good negotiators, who are not afraid to ask for the moon on your behalf.

Whenever I purchase a rental property, I ask my agents to have the sellers to pick up the cost of a home warranty and assume 2% or 3% of the closing cost, or the maximum that FHA will allow. The home warranty will come in handy down the road, if you have to repair the furnace, AC unit, water heater, stove, or refrigerator.

3. You need a couple **good mortgage brokers** who are attuned to the market, and who have several lenders to get you the best interest rates possible. Depending on the type of real estate deal you're putting together, you need a broker who is creative, and who can structure the deal to avoid rejection from the underwriters. I'm fortunate to have two such Brokers on my team. Tony Williams and Amy Wulf. Amy is a five-star broker. I always tease her by saying that she's earning her sixth star! She's one of the very best in the business.

4. You need a **good <u>handy-man</u> or <u>handy-woman</u>** who is knowledgeable, skilled at doing minor repairs, and who is available when you call. Please develop a good relationship with this person. They can save you lots of money, preventing you from getting ripped off by shady contractors and they can help alleviate lots of your potential headaches.

5. You need a couple **good heating and cooling technicians** who will accept payments from your home warranty companies, give you a fair price for their labor, and who are readily available when it's 3 degrees outside and one of your furnaces stop working. Or when it's 99 degrees outside and an AC unit, or the compressor fails to work.

6. You need a couple **good electricians and plumbers** who are readily available and who are knowledgeable about building codes in the municipalities that your properties are located. It helps if they know and have a relationship with the respective inspectors in your area. Those relationships come in handy when you need your property to pass inspection!

7. You need a couple **good contractors** who do good major repairs and are knowledgeable about building codes in your area and will give you a fair price for their labor. The good ones are always busy, so it's important to establish a good relationship with them, in the event that you need them to evaluate a property, or give you an estimate.

8. Finally, you need a **good tree-trimming, tree removal, and landscaping guy**, who will respond to your call immediately after the storm to remove tree branches from your properties. Again, establish a good relationship with this guy, so that he will give you a fair price and respond to you quickly.

Meet our Five Star Real-Estate Team

Ms. Amy Wulf
5 Star Mortgage Broker
awulf@usa-mortgage.com

Ms. Robin Howard
Owner, Robin's Nest Really
robin@robinsnestrealty.net

Ms. Debbie Weber
5 Star Real-Estate Agent
debbieweber@kw.com

Mr. Tony Williams
Mortgage Loan Officer
tonywilliams842@gmail.com

Mr. Wes Villhard, PE
Owner, House Master Home Inspections
wes.villhard@housemaster.com

Mr. Rodney McCain
Owner, Green Jacket Lawn Care, LLC
greenjacklc@gmail.com

Mr. Rick Morgan
Handyman

Not Pictured:

Mr. MO Kelly, Owner & Contractor
VIP Painting & Remodeling

Mr. Anthony Young
Electrician

Mr. Scotty Anderson, Owner
Scottie Anderson HVAC

Mr. Aristeed Harris, Owner
Harris Heating & Cooling

Mr. Harold Edwards
Plumber

Chapter 18

RECAPPING

1. Start with **homeownership**. Stop renting and making your landlord wealthy. Improve your FICO scores and your credit scores, so that you can purchase that 1st home, and save some cash. You will also need good credit in order to invest in rentals, or to secure cash for your startup business.

2. Buy a single-family home and start **building equity** (Another name for wealth)

3. To speed up the process, **buy a 2-family home**, rent one unit and live in the other unit rent free, thereby saving almost your entire paycheck!

4. With the money you save, **buy more** single or 2-family **homes**, preferably 3 and 2s (units with 3 bedrooms and 2 bathrooms.) You can rent them to Section-8 Families *all day long*! (Be sure to screen your tenants well.) Your rental income is called **passive income**.

5. Add some **residual income** by seeking a career or investments that provide it. (Become an insurance agent, an insurance broker, author, movie maker, or ATM owner. You can also purchase stocks that pay dividends and receive residual income. This is money you receive on all of your sales every month without having to do anything. Those checks keep coming!

6. Add some **stock market income** by investing money from your passive and residual income, in the stock market. Remember, if you:

a) Place you money under the mattress - Your ROI (rate of return) is $0
(b) Place it in the Bank - Your ROI is .5%
(c) Purchase Municipal Bonds - Your ROI is 6% to 7%
(d) Purchase Stocks – You'll Average 10%+ depending on the economy.

7. Consider being **self-employed**. Take control of your most important asset, your time! You can take a nap, ride your bike, or play a round of golf in the middle of the day, if that's what you want to do. You can go on vacation and return whenever you want.

8. Consider **starting a business**. Blacks need more businesses. If it's successful, you can employ family members and pass it on to future generations, thereby creating generational wealth and lowering black unemployment.

9. Purchase **term insurance** to protect your major assets (your personal home and your rental properties) throughout the loan period. Each 30-year mortgage should be protected by a 30-year term policy (for the same amount of the mortgage plus interest.) If you or your spouse should pass within that 30-year loan period, the insurance proceeds would pay off the remaining loan, so that the other spouse now owns the house free and clear.

10. Purchase **whole life insurance** when you're young for your final expense (Your burial.) As you age, the premiums will remain the same.

11. Secure **your family's land** with the appropriate titles and deeds, so that you can pass it on to future generations! God's not making any *more land* on earth. At some point, the only land that may be available, may be land on the Moon or on Mars!

12. Create **wills and trusts** so that you can correctly pass on your assets to your loved ones, ensuring generational wealth.

13. If you own a home, and was unable to build wealth during your working career, **consider a reverse mortgage**, to pull some of that equity out so that you can use it to enjoy your remaining years on earth! Be sure to back it up with a term insurance policy and an interest-bearing security like a municipal bond, or dividend-paying Stocks, that will provide income to cover the monthly premiums on the insurance policy. When you pass, the term insurance proceeds will pay off the reverse mortgage loan, so that your loved ones will own your home, free and clear (and not the government!)

14. If you're faced with foreclosure proceedings, and you're 62 years of age or older, again **consider a reverse mortgage.** It will pay off your mortgage, allowing you to avoid foreclosure. Depending on the equity in your home, you may even be able to pull some $ cash out, to buy a used car, to go on a cruise, or to go on a Nice Vacation – where you can sit on the beach and sip on a cocktail while you ponder how you "dodged a bullet"!

15. **Be cautious of taking out student loans**. They could burden you with a whole lot of **unnecessary debt**, raising your DTI ratio (Debt to income ratio) preventing you from purchasing homes, or borrowing money to start your business. Ultimately derailing your wealth building strategies.

16. Pay Your Taxes! – Tax liens can prevent you from borrowing the money you will need to build your wealth.

17. Finally, **consider becoming a mentor.** Please don't keep this knowledge to yourself. Pass it on to: your children, your grandchildren, your neighbor's children, your church members, your sororities and fraternities, your local high schools, your local community colleges, and universities. You have an obligation to **spread this knowledge**, so that we can finally end generational Black poverty and **replace it with generational Black wealth**!

Chapter - 19

Giving Back by Becoming a Black Mentor

Unfortunately, our schools and our colleges and universities teach very little of what we discussed in this book. As a result, it's incumbent upon every black adult to do our part to spread the word. We have to impart this wisdom and these life lessons on our children, to help end the cycle of black poverty, and to help build generational black wealth.

The sooner our children learn about money, how to save it, invest it, and manage it, the sooner they will be on a path to success. The sooner our children learn about credit (good and bad) and FICO scores, the sooner they will make good decisions that will have a significant impact on their lives. The sooner they understand the importance and impact of leverage, the sooner they will make power moves toward building wealth.

How, when and where should we teach our children this vitally important Information? This book was written in a very simplistic manner, in order that children and seniors can read it and understand what they're reading. The information is so important that we should start at home. If you have young children, make it a family event and read it out loud to them, and ask questions as you cover certain topics that may be new to them. If you're not familiar with a certain term or topic in this book, please Google it!

Get another explanation or perspective that will bring clarity to the topic. Call a friend or family member and ask questions and discuss it with them.

Every junior high, high school, and college-age black student, should read this book. High school black Students, who are getting ready to apply to colleges and universities, should specifically read chapter 5 (The Student Loan SCAM) before applying for student loans, and taking on an enormous amount of unnecessary debt that can ruin their lives, and "**Stop Them From Building Wealth**".

If you have no children, you're not off the hook! Please reach out to your nieces and nephews, please volunteer at your local schools, your churches, your fraternities and sororities, your local chapter of the NAACP, the Urban League, and the 100 Black Men.

Contact your local schools, bookstores, and libraries. Make sure that they have adequate supplies of *this* important book. If they question your motives or your concerns, please explain to them the byproducts of poverty: crime, mental illness, poor health, homelessness, unemployment, and hunger! Enough said!

Building wealth is not rocket science! Anyone (young, old, Black, White, Hispanic) can use the simple steps provided in this book, to build wealth.

BIOGRAPHY

During the '60s and my early childhood in Barbados, I was fortunate to witness my parents' entrepreneurial spirit. My dad was an executive at a sugar factory during the week, while my mom ran our family's dry-cleaning business (Millers Laundry) on Baxter's Road in Bridgetown, Barbados. On weekends, my mom (an accomplished seamstress) made outfits for family and friends, while my dad (an accomplished tailor) also made suits and slacks. I grew up learning how to build wealth (thanks to my parents) at a very early age. It became a part of my DNA. I also passed that knowledge onto my children at a very early age, and they in-turn will do the same with their children. I learned how to save at the age of 10 when I opened my first savings account. At 14 when I got my first real job in New York, I wasn't pleased with the interest on the savings account, so I learned how to invest and how to seek a bigger ROI (return on investment). Around that time, I also learned the importance of good credit and the leverage that comes with it.

I went to Junior High School 136 in the Bronx and Theodore Roosevelt High School also in the Bronx. Then, I attended the City College of New York where I received an Undergraduate degree in Economics, and I received my MBA from Long Island University. Throughout my entire educational experience, not once do I recall any of my teachers or professors discussing any of the vitally important topics in this book, such as: FICO scores, good credit, passive income, residual income, investing in the stock market, or estate planning.

I'm not alone in this regard. Most of my family members and friends never received this vitally important information from their schools and universities either. How on Earth could educators fail to teach such important information?

Was this omission intentional? Why was it not included in our curriculums? As a society, if we're serious about **ending poverty**, and ending the by products of poverty: crime, mental illness, poor health, homelessness, unemployment, and hunger! Why would we fail to teach people how to build wealth?

72

Therein lies the reasons why I wrote *Building Black Wealth*. I've been fortunate to receive this knowledge, and it has definitely served me well throughout my lifetime. As a result, I felt the need to share the information with folks who look like me.

Over the years, I've owned several businesses including: an automobile dealership (Accent Lincoln Mercury in St Louis, Missouri), an insurance agency which I currently own and operate in St Louis, Missouri (StoneLeaf Finance & Insurance Group – www.stoneleafinsurance.com), an internet marketing company (Automotive Internet Marketing), an internet portal (AutoconsultantsUSA.com), and a real-estate company that currently manages our rental properties. I've also been self-employed for several years as an insurance broker.

Throughout my business career, I've learned the importance of having multiple revenue streams: residual income, passive income and stock market income are the three I focus on in this book. My first business (the Automobile Dealership) was very cyclical. Sales and profits were off in September when my clients focused on back to school supplies. Thanksgiving and Christmas were always slow, when they focused on the Holidays. During recessions, it got even worst with unemployment skyrocketing. As a result, I had to seek my income from business ventures that were **recession proof** to eliminate the peaks and valleys in my revenue. Real-estate and insurance foot the bill perfectly. People always need shelter! When they get paid, they make it a point to pay rent, life insurance, health insurance, car insurance, and home insurance first even before buying food.

The lessons I've learned over the years, the experience of running several businesses and being self-employed have all contributed to the knowledge shared with you in this book. The hope is that you will use it to build your wealth, and that you will share it with your family, friends, and loved ones, so that together, **we *will* build generational black wealth!**

Thank you for reading *BUILDING BLACK WEALTH.*

African American Home Ownership Statistics

Home Ownership is the first step in building
"Generational Black Wealth"

"In 1936, Tai Christensen's great grandmother, a housekeeper and widow in North Carolina with 4 sons, saved up $500 and bought a house at age 35. That decision, changed the trajectory of her family's finances for generations to come".[15]

"Today homeownership rates of black people lag even further behind whites' rates, affecting their ability to build wealth".

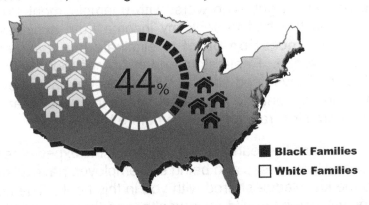

■ **Black Families**
□ **White Families**

1. In the first quarter of 2020, 44% of black families owned their home, compared to 73.7% of whites which is the widest gap in US cities with more than 1 million residents.

2. Only 50% of black families own their home in Washington, DC, which has the highest homeownership rate in the

U.S., versus more than 70% of white families. Nationwide the gap is 44% versus 73.7%.

3. Just 25% of black families in Minneapolis, own homes. The lowest black homeownership rate of any metro area in the U.S. with more than 1 million residents. It's followed by Milwaukee at 27%, and Salt Lake City at 28%.

How Redlining Contributed to a racial wealth gap.[16]

Redlining, the racist housing policy that was outlawed in the 1960s, remains a major factor in today's wealth gap between Black and white families across the country. The typical homeowner in a neighborhood that was redlined for mortgage lending by the federal government has gained 52% less—or $212,023 less—in personal wealth generated by property value increases than one in a greenlined neighborhood over the last 40 years. Black homeowners are nearly five times more likely to own in a formerly redlined neighborhood than in a greenlined neighborhood, resulting in diminished home equity and overall economic inequality for Black families.

In Type A Neighborhoods, the Homeownership Gap Between Black and White Families Expands

In the 41 metros included in this analysis, Black individuals who are homeowners are 4.7 times as likely to own in a former Type D than a Type A neighborhood, while white individuals are just 1.5 times more likely to own in a redlined area. And even though redlining was outlawed half a century ago, the homeownership rate for Black families has dropped in every neighborhood type over the last 40 years.

Since 1980, the homeownership rate for Black families in Type A, or "best," neighborhoods dropped from 50.4% to just 44.0%, while the rate for white families rose 4.1 percentage points to 71% in 2017, the most recent data that was available at the time of the analysis for this report. That makes for a 27 percentage-point homeownership gap between Black and white families in "best" neighborhoods, up from a 16.5 percentage-point gap

40 years ago. The gap has widened in all neighborhood types except those that were formerly redlined, where Black and white families both have relatively low homeownership rates (29.8% and 45.6%, respectively).

Black homeowners were hit harder during the 2008 housing bust, with 7.9% of Black families with mortgages losing their homes to foreclosure between 2007 and 2009 versus 4.5% of white families, and it's likely that the subsequent tightening of credit has been an exacerbating factor in the homeownership gap.

Homeownership Rates by Race and Redlining Category:

National

In some areas, the difference is more pronounced. The homeownership rate for Type A areas in Atlantic City, NJ is just 14.8% for Black families, versus 75.3% for white families. That's a bigger gap than any other metro. It's followed by Fresno, CA, where the Type A homeownership rate for Black families is just 2.5% compared to 62.6% for white families, and Greensboro, NC (9.3% versus 67.7%). The homeownership gap for "best" neighborhoods is smallest in Oakland, where Black families have an 84.1% homeownership rate versus 85.9% for white families. It's followed by Miami (42.7% versus 56.8%).

How redlining contributed to a racial wealth gap.
Statistics provided by REDFIN News
Published on June, 11 2020 – by Dana Anderson

Opportunities:

Despite redlining, and credit challenges, homeownership is still the best way for blacks to build wealth, and pass that wealth on to our children and our grandchildren. With low interest rates and stock market gains, this is a perfect time to purchase homes for personal use and for investments.

EXAMPLES OF HOME APPRECIATION – INCREASED EQUITY (WEALTH)

Example | House – A: In June of 2019, I purchased this single family (3 bed/3 baths) home for $65,000 as an investment rental. In Oct 2021 it was appraised for $100,000 so in December of 2021, I pulled $30,000 Equity out, and paid off the mortgage on House - C (which I purchased for $45,000 and now own free & clear)

Example | House – B: In August of 2020, I purchased this single family (3 beds/ 2 baths) home for $60,000 as an investment rental property. In October 2021, it now has a Zestimate value of $75,000, with a Zestimate range of $69,000 to $82,000. That's $20,000+ Equity in a little over 1 year.

Example | House – C: In December 2020, I purchased this (3 beds/ 2 bath) home for $45,000 as an investment rental property. In December 2021, I paid off the existing mortgage and now own it <u>free & clear</u>, while collecting that monthly rental income.

•

Eventually, <u>I will payoff all</u> of my Rental Mortgages, with: <u>the equity they</u> <u>gained</u>, or with "<u>House Money</u>" from my <u>Stock Market Gains</u>, while continuing to collect the rental income from each property.

BIBLIOGRAPHY

1. "Special Field Order No. 15," Wikipedia. 17 July 2021, https://en.wikipedia.org/wiki/Special_Field_Orders_No._15

2. "FICO," *my*FICO.com 2001-2021, https://www.myfico.com/consumer-division-of-fico.aspx

3. "2021 FHA Loan Eligibility," FHA*loans*.com - A Mortgage Research Center, LLC Network Website. 2021, https://www.fhaloans.com/lp/?utm_campaign=national&utm_source=bing&utm_medium=cpc&src=msn&adg=mf-hareq&desc=eligibility3&msclkid=388d3fa622171b-cb94ee5efe30989d73&utm_term=fha%20loan%20requirements&utm_content=Requirements.

4. "What is Debt to Income Ratio?", Zillow. 2006-2021, https://www.zillow.com/mortgage-learning/debt-to-income-ratio/?msclkid=2c0c1711cc611758a10a7649df8a49fc&sem-Que=dti%20ratio%20formula&1310618117792782kwd-81913785043900:loc-19081913695057098.

5. Miller, Rich. *Dealing.* 2020

6. PMI (Private Mortgage Insurance) Calculator, NerdWallet. 2021, https://www.nerdwallet.com/article/mortgages/pmi-calculator?trk_location=ssrp&trk_query=pmi%20calculator&trk_page=1&trk_position=2.

7. Janet Berry-Johnson, "The Big List of Small Business Tax Deductions," Bench. 30 July 2021, https://bench.co/blog/tax-tips/small-business-tax-deductions/.

8. "Student Loan Debt," Nitro College. 2021, https://www.nitrocollege.com/research/average-student-loan-debt

9. "Digest of Education" (Estimated Average Annual Salary of Teachers), National Center for Education Statistics. 1970-2020, https://nces.ed.gov/programs/digest/d20/tables/dt20_211.60.asp

10. "Occupational Outlook Handbook" (Average National Social Worker Salary), Bureau of Labor Statistics. 8 September 2021, https://www.bls.gov/ooh/community-and-social-service/social-workers.htm

11. Ben Davis, "What is the average rate of return on municipal bonds?," Mv Organizing. 17 April 2019, https://www.mvorganizing.org/what-is-the-average-rate-of-return-on-municipal-bonds/#:~:text=What%20is%20the%20average%20rate%20of%20return%20on,maturity%20now%20range%20between%202%25%20and%202.25%25.%20

12. "Silk Road," Wikipedia. 29 September 2021, https://en.wikipedia.org/wiki/Silk_Road_(marketplace)

13. Maggie and John Anderson, *Our Black Year: One Family's Quest to Buy Black in America's Racially Divided Economy*, 2012.

14. Tom Huddleston Jr., "Black Wall Street: The history of the wealthy black community and the massacre perpetrated there 100 years ago", CNBC. 28 May 2021, https://www.cnbc.com/2020/07/04/what-is-black-wall-street-history-of-the-community-and-its-massacre.html

15. Michele Lerner, "African American Homeownership," Statistics, Washington Post. 23 July 2020

16. Dana Anderson, Redlining's Legacy of Inequality: $212,000 Less Home Equity, Low Homeownership Rates for Black Families, Redfin. 15 October 2020, https://www.redfin.com/news/redlining-real-estate-racial-wealth-gap/

Richard A. Miller - Author

Richard A. Miller with family

NOTES:

NOTES:

NOTES:

NOTES:

NOTES:

NOTES:

NOTES:

NOTES:

NOTES:

NOTES:

NOTES:

NOTES:

CONTACTS:

CONTACTS:

CONTACTS:

CONTACTS:

Made in the USA
Monee, IL
10 February 2024

52766066R00066